ALBANIA 2016 HUMAN RIGHTS REPORT

EXECUTIVE SUMMARY

The Republic of Albania is a parliamentary democracy. The constitution vests legislative authority in the unicameral parliament (the Assembly), which elects both the prime minister and the president. The prime minister heads the government, while the president has limited executive power. In June 2015 the country held local elections for mayors and municipal councils. The Organization for Security and Cooperation in Europe (OSCE) assessed the elections positively overall but observed important procedural irregularities. In 2013 the country held parliamentary elections that the OSCE reported were competitive and respected fundamental freedoms but were conducted in an atmosphere of distrust that tainted the electoral environment.

Civilian authorities maintained effective control over the security forces.

The most significant human rights problems were pervasive corruption in all branches of government, particularly in the judicial and health-care systems, and domestic violence and discrimination against women.

Other human rights problems included significantly substandard prison and detention center conditions, notably overcrowded, aged infrastructure, with a lack of medical treatment for inmates. Reportedly, police and prison guards sometimes beat and abused suspects and detainees and occasionally held persons in prolonged detention without charge. Political pressure, intimidation, widespread corruption, and limited resources sometimes prevented the judiciary from functioning independently and efficiently. The government made little progress in addressing the many claims for the return or restitution of property seized during the Communist era. Authorities demolished homes and businesses without due legal process or recourse for owners to receive adequate compensation. Government, business, and criminal groups sought to influence media in inappropriate ways, and there were reports of violence and intimidation against members of the media. Journalists often practiced self-censorship to avoid violence and harassment and as a response to pressure from publishers and editors. There continued to be indications of widespread child abuse. Forced and early marriage was a problem in some parts of the country. There were many displaced children and street children, particularly within the Romani community. The country continued to be a source and destination for men, women, and children subjected to sex trafficking and forced labor. Marginalization and abuse of the Romani and Balkan-Egyptian communities were serious problems, as was discrimination based on sexual orientation and gender identity. Government enforcement of labor laws remained weak and rarely protected domestic and migrant workers. Large numbers of children were engaged in forced labor. There were reports of employment discrimination based on gender, disability, sexual orientation or gender identity, nationality, and ethnicity.

Impunity remained a problem. Prosecution, and especially conviction, of officials who committed abuses was sporadic and inconsistent. Officials, politicians, judges, and those with powerful business interests often were able to avoid prosecution. Authorities took technical measures, such as electronic payment of traffic fines, to improve police accountability and punished some lower-level officials for abuses.

Section 1. Respect for the Integrity of the Person, Including Freedom from:

a. Arbitrary Deprivation of Life and other Unlawful or Politically Motivated Killings

There were no reports that the government or its agents committed arbitrary or unlawful killings.

b. Disappearance

There were no reports of politically motivated disappearances.

c. Torture and Other Cruel, Inhuman, or Degrading Treatment or Punishment

While the constitution and law prohibit such actions, police and prison guards sometimes beat and abused suspects and detainees. Through September the Service for Internal Affairs and Complaints received complaints of police abuse and corruption that led to both administrative sanctions and criminal prosecutions.

On March 3, the Council of Europe's Committee for the Prevention of Torture (CPT) released its report on its most recent visit to the country in 2014. As in 2010, the CPT reported receiving a significant number of credible reports from detained persons, including juveniles, of physical mistreatment by police officers, consisting mainly of slaps, punches, kicks, and truncheon blows.

Through September the ombudsman received 140 complaints from detainees. Nearly one quarter of the complaints alleged physical or psychological abuse; the office of the ombudsman forwarded three of these to prosecutors.

Prison and Detention Center Conditions

Lack of medical treatment, particularly for mental health issues, was a serious problem, as were overcrowded facilities and poor physical infrastructure. The Albanian Helsinki Committee (AHC) reported that conditions in certain detention facilities were so poor as to constitute inhuman treatment. Authorities improved some police detention facilities as part of a nationwide upgrade, but conditions remained poor outside of Tirana and other major urban centers. AHC research conducted among inmates through July showed the majority of complaints centered on poor living conditions, interference with private correspondence with family members, unresponsiveness to prisoner complaints and requests, delayed transfer of detainees from police stations to detention facilities, as well as physical or psychological abuse by prison staff or other inmates. As of July, six cases, or approximately 11 percent of all complaints, alleged physical or psychological abuse.

Physical Conditions: The prison population was on average 9 percent greater than the design capacity of prison facilities. Overcrowding was especially serious in pretrial detention centers. Conditions in prison and detention centers for women were generally better than those for men.

The government reported 12 deaths in prison through August; 10 were from natural causes, one from a fire incident in the Lezha Prison, and one from suicide. On July 30, a Lezha prison cell caught fire, resulting in the death of one inmate and the injury of five others and two guards. The General Directorate of Prisons fired 11 employees and disciplined 21 others as a result. On July 31, an inmate at Vaqarr prison was shot and injured in the prison yard. The inmate received medical assistance; the investigation continued at year's end.

The majority of the 140 complaints received by the ombudsman from detainees through September dealt with the quality of health services. Detainees also complained about access to special leave programs, delays in the implementation of prison transfer orders, and undesirable transfers to other prisons. The AHC also reported an increased number of complaints about the quality of health services as well as transfer/nontransfer between detention facilities. The ombudsman and nongovernmental organizations (NGOs) reported that authorities detained inmates with mental disabilities in regular prisons, where access to mental health care was wholly inadequate.

Prison and detention center conditions varied significantly by age and type of facility. The AHC identified problems in both new and old structures, such as dampness in cells, poor hygiene, lack of bedding materials, and inconsistent water supply.

Conditions in facilities operated by the Ministry of Interior, such as police stations and temporary detention facilities, were inadequate, except for regional facilities in Tirana, Durres, Gjirokaster, and Korca, which the government renovated in 2014 and 2015. Most detention facilities were unheated during the winter. Some lacked basic hygienic amenities, such as showers or sinks. Facilities were cramped, afforded limited access to toilets, and had little or no ventilation, natural light, or beds and benches.

Administration: The Ministry of Justice managed the country's prisons. The ombudsman reported prison and police officials generally cooperated with investigations. NGOs and the ombudsman noted inadequate recordkeeping in some institutions, particularly in small or rural police stations.

Corruption continued to be a serious problem in detention centers, particularly in connection with access to work and special release programs. NGOs reported that those involved in work programs received less than 125 leks (one dollar) per month and did not receive credit for social security.

Independent Monitoring: The government allowed local and international human rights groups, the media, as well as international bodies such as the CPT to monitor prison conditions. The ombudsman conducted frequent unannounced inspections of detention facilities. In September the ombudsman reportedly was denied access to Fier prison to investigate claims of violence against an inmate.

Improvements: During the year the ombudsman and NGOs reported improvements in conditions in some prisons and detention centers. The General Directorate of Prisons indicated that by July overall prison overcrowding had been reduced from 25 percent over full capacity in 2015 to 9 percent. NGOs reported that police and prison authorities continued to demonstrate greater sensitivity toward the rights of juvenile and female detainees. The ombudsman noted that authorities were more flexible in allowing juveniles in pretrial detention centers to meet with relatives. Tirana's Jordan Misja detention facility, which closed in 2015 after the ombudsman deemed it unsuitable, reopened with substantially improved living conditions.

d. Arbitrary Arrest or Detention

The law and constitution prohibit arbitrary arrest and detention, and the government generally observed these prohibitions.

Role of the Police and Security Apparatus

The Ministry of Interior oversees the State Police, the Guard of the Republic, and the Border and Migration Police. The State Police are primarily responsible for internal security. The Guard of the Republic protects senior state officials, foreign dignitaries, and certain state properties. The Ministry of Defense oversees the armed forces, which also assist the population in times of humanitarian need. The State Intelligence Service (SIS) gathers information, carries out foreign intelligence and counterintelligence activities, and is responsible to the prime minister.

Civilian authorities generally maintained effective control over police, the Guard of the Republic, the armed forces, and the SIS, although officials periodically used state resources for personal gain and members of the security forces committed abuses.

Police did not always enforce the law equitably. Personal associations, political or criminal connections, poor infrastructure, lack of equipment, or inadequate supervision often influenced law enforcement. Low salaries, poor motivation and leadership, and a lack of diversity in the workforce contributed to continued corruption and unprofessional behavior. Authorities made efforts to address these problems by renovating police facilities, upgrading vehicles, introducing the use of in-car and body cameras, and publicly highlighting anticorruption measures.

Impunity remained a serious problem, although the government made greater efforts to address it, in particular by increasing the use of camera evidence to document and prosecute police misconduct. In April the Supreme Court upheld the one and three-year sentences handed down, respectively, to Guards of the Republic Ndrea Prendi and Agim Llupo, charged in the 2011 killings of four protesters.

While the government had mechanisms to investigate and punish abuse and corruption, police corruption remained a problem. The Service for Internal Affairs and Complaints conducted audits, responded to complaints, and carried out investigations with increased emphasis on human rights, prison conditions, and adherence to standard operating procedures. This office fielded 2,202 complaints, including 1,777 phone calls via the anticorruption "green line." As of September authorities dealt with 34 cases involving 46 officers as administrative violations and handled eight cases involving eight officers as criminal offenses, forwarding them for prosecution. During the year the ombudsman also processed complaints against police officers, mainly relating to problems with arrests and detention.

Since 2014 the government has increased police salaries and instituted an open competition for new recruits, although the Albanian Security Academy reportedly exerted inappropriate influence over police hiring, firing, and promotions. Police were not compliant with special orders mandating women comprise 50 percent of new recruits, with the goal of reaching 30 percent female representation across the police force. The March appointment of a diversity specialist increased senior-level attention to the problem.

Arrest Procedures and Treatment of Detainees

The law requires that, except for arrests made during the commission of a crime, police may arrest a suspect on criminal grounds only with a warrant issued by a judge and based on sufficient evidence. There were no reports of secret arrests. By law police must immediately inform the prosecutor of an arrest. The prosecutor may release the suspect or petition the court within 48 hours to hold the individual further. A court must decide within 48 hours whether to place a suspect in detention, require bail, prohibit travel, or require the defendant to report regularly to the police. Prosecutors requested, and courts ordered, detention in many criminal cases, although courts sometimes denied prosecutors' requests for detention of well-connected, high-profile defendants.

The constitution requires authorities to inform detained persons immediately of the charges against them and their rights. Law enforcement authorities did not always respect this requirement. There was no effective system for handling the monetary aspect of bail. Instead, courts often ordered suspects to report to police or prosecutors on a weekly basis. While the law gives detainees the right to prompt access to an attorney, at public expense if necessary, NGOs reported interrogations often took place without the presence of a lawyer. Authorities placed many suspects under house arrest, often at their own request, because if convicted they received credit for time served.

By law police should transfer detainees to the custody of the Ministry of Justice, which has facilities more appropriate for long-term detention, if their custody will exceed 10 hours. Due to overcrowding in the penitentiary system, detainees, including juveniles, commonly remained in police detention centers for long periods.

<u>Arbitrary Arrest</u>: The constitution and law prohibit arbitrary arrest and detention. Although the government generally observed these prohibitions, there were instances when police detained persons for questioning for inordinate lengths of time without formally arresting them.

<u>Pretrial Detention</u>: While the law requires completion of most pretrial investigations within three months, a prosecutor may extend this period to two years or longer. The law provides that pretrial detention should not exceed three years; the government reported seven cases of pretrial detentions exceeding this limit. Extended pretrial detention often occurred due to delayed investigations, defense mistakes, or the intentional failure of defense counsel to appear. By law a judge cannot prevent such delaying actions by holding the offending attorney in contempt of court. Limited material resources, lack of space, poor court-calendar management, insufficient staff, and failure of attorneys and witnesses to appear prevented the court system from adjudicating cases in a timely fashion. As of September, approximately half of the prison and detention center population was in pretrial detention.

<u>Detainee's Ability to Challenge Lawfulness of Detention before a Court</u>: The criminal procedure code requires that the court examine the necessity of a detention within three days. If the detention is not revoked, the detainee may appeal up to the Supreme Court. If no decision is made within a prescribed period, the detention becomes void. The criminal procedure code also requires the prosecutor to provide the court bi-monthly updates regarding information obtained following detention. This includes providing summaries of testimonial and documentary evidence received. If warranted, the judge may revoke the detention based on the new information.

<u>Protracted Detention of Rejected Asylum Seekers or Stateless Persons</u>: Authorities often detained irregular migrants who entered the country. By September authorities had detained approximately 500 migrants at the country's southern

border with Greece; those who did not request asylum were deported to Greece within 24 hours. Migrants detained further inland generally spent up to a month at the Karrec migrant detention facility awaiting deportation. The Office of the UN High Commissioner for Refugees (UNHCR) could monitor the processing, detention, and deportation of migrants. The government reported that less than 10 percent of migrants requested asylum, although NGOs maintained that some migrants who requested asylum might have been deported as well. UNHCR reported that conditions at the Karrec center were unsuitable, particularly for children. In August the government began moving some migrants to the Babrru open migrant facility, where conditions were better.

e. Denial of Fair Public Trial

Although the constitution provides for an independent judiciary, political pressure, intimidation, widespread corruption, and limited resources sometimes prevented the judiciary from functioning independently and efficiently. Court hearings were often not open to the public. Court security officers frequently refused to admit observers to hearings and routinely telephoned the presiding judge to ask whether to admit an individual seeking to attend a particular hearing. Some agencies exhibited a pattern of disregard for court orders. The politicization of appointments to the Supreme Court and Constitutional Court threatened to undermine the independence and integrity of these institutions. As of September, two vacancies in the Supreme Court remained unfilled after nearly three years, despite a considerable backlog of cases facing the court.

The Ministry of Justice generally did not vigorously pursue disciplinary measures against judges. When it did so, the High Council of Justice was reluctant to enact those measures. Through October the ministry had initiated disciplinary proceedings against eight judges. Of these, authorities dismissed one, suspended another, and transferred one to a different jurisdiction. At the request of the Prosecutor General's Office, the High Court also ordered the suspension of a High Court judge. This judge was later charged with receiving a bribe, and the case was pending at year's end.

Trial Procedures

The law presumes defendants to be innocent until convicted. It provides for defendants to be informed promptly and in detail of the charges against them, with free interpretation as necessary, and to have a fair and public trial without undue delay. Defendants have the right to be present at their trial, consult an attorney and have one provided at public expense if they cannot afford one. The law provides defendants adequate time and facilities to prepare a defense, access to interpretation free of charge, and the right to access government-held evidence. Defendants have the right to confront witnesses against them and to present witnesses and evidence in their defense. Defendants may not be compelled to testify or confess guilt. Defendants have the right to appeal. The government generally respected these rights, although trials were not always public and access to a lawyer was at times problematic. Despite the statutory right to free legal aid, NGOs reported that very few individuals benefitted from this during the year.

Political Prisoners and Detainees

There were no reports of political prisoners or detainees.

Civil Judicial Procedures and Remedies

While individuals and organizations may seek civil remedies for human rights violations, courts were susceptible to corruption, inefficiency, intimidation, and political tampering. Judges held many court hearings in their offices, demonstrating a lack of professionalism and providing opportunities for corruption. These factors undermined the judiciary's authority, contributed to controversial court decisions, and led to an inconsistent application of civil law.

Persons who have exhausted remedies in domestic courts could appeal to the European Court of Human Rights (ECHR). As of September, 495 cases were pending before the ECHR, most related to nonenforcement of domestic judicial or administrative decisions. In many instances, authorities did not enforce ECHR rulings. A 2013 study by the Open Society Foundation for Albania--Soros Foundation found that lawyers, prosecutors, and judges had limited knowledge of ECHR jurisprudence.

Persons who were political prisoners under the former communist regime continued to petition the government for compensation. On several occasions, groups of former political prisoners protested the government's failure to pay them legally mandated compensation. The law gives priority to compensating women, the elderly, those with serious illnesses, and those who had never received a payment. The government made some progress on disbursing compensation during the year.

Property Restitution

Thousands of claims for private and religious property confiscated during the communist era remained unresolved with the government's Agency for Property Treatment. Claimants may appeal cases to the ECHR and during the year hundreds of cases--many of them related to property--were pending review there.

f. Arbitrary or Unlawful Interference with Privacy, Family, Home, or Correspondence

The government's National Inspectorate for the Protection of the Territory (NIPT) demolished some homes without due legal process as part of a wider campaign to demolish illegally constructed buildings. Through August the ombudsman received 16 citizen complaints against the NIPT, including failure to provide sufficient warning in writing, failure to consider a homeowner's application for legalization of a property, and carelessness resulting in damage to other personal property, such as furniture and other structures.

Throughout the year residents of the Himara region complained of targeted heavy-handedness by the government that resulted in the partial or entire demolition of numerous houses and business with little warning and no legal recourse for adequate compensation. Authorities said the demolitions were needed for commercial development and cultural preservation. Residents claimed the government often did not recognize legal documentation of ownership and dispossessed home and landowners with minimal financial compensation.

Section 2. Respect for Civil Liberties, Including:

a. Freedom of Speech and Press

The constitution provides for freedom of speech and press, and the government generally respected these rights. There were reports that the government, business, and criminal groups sought to influence the media in inappropriate ways.

Press and Media Freedoms: Independent media were active and expressed a wide variety of viewpoints, although there were some efforts to exert direct and indirect political and economic pressure on the media, including threats and violence against journalists who tried to investigate crime and corruption stories. Political pressure, corruption, and lack of funding constrained the independent print media, and journalists reportedly practiced self-censorship.

Online media saw a dramatic growth during the year, which added to the diversity of views. According to 2015 estimates, approximately 15 percent of the country's 1,500 reporters worked in online media outlets.

In its annual *Media Sustainability Index*, the International Research and Exchanges Board indicated that the economic crisis continued to erode the independence of the media. At least one major newspaper closed for financial reasons. Funding for organizations that pushed for a more independent press remained limited, and the press was vulnerable to misuse under constant political and economic pressure.

The majority of citizens received their news from television and radio. The independence of the Audiovisual Media Authority, the regulator of the broadcast media market, remained questionable. The role of the authority remained limited, even after its board was fully staffed in mid-year.

In May the Constitutional Court decided in favor of a petition by the Albanian Electronic Media Association to abrogate a law that prevented an individual shareholder from owning more than a 40 percent share in a national broadcast media outlet. Some observers viewed the decision as paving the way to the potential monopolization of the already small number of national digital broadcast licenses. The EU, the Council of Europe, and the OSCE had previously criticized a 2015 attempt by the Assembly to annul the same article.

While private television stations generally operated free of direct government influence, most owners used the content of their broadcasts to influence government action toward their other businesses. Business owners also freely used media outlets to gain favor and promote their interests with political parties.

<u>Violence and Harassment</u>: There were reports of violence and intimidation against members of the media, and political and business interests subjected journalists to pressure. Intimidation of journalists through social media continued.

On May 9, the Union of Albanian Journalists denounced the severe beating of sports journalist Eduard Ilnica, allegedly for reporting on the violent behavior of a coach during a soccer match. Authorities arrested the coach and released him on bail. There were reports that Ilnica decided not to press charges after reaching a private agreement with the defendant, but the prosecutor's office took the case to court; a trial was pending.

<u>Censorship or Content Restrictions</u>: Journalists often practiced self-censorship to avoid violence and harassment and as a response to pressure from publishers and editors seeking to advance their political and economic interests. A 2015 survey by the Balkan Investigative Regional Network Albania found that large commercial companies and important advertisers were key sources of pressure. Lack of economic security reduced reporters' independence and contributed to bias in reporting. Albanian journalist unions continued to report significant delays in salary payments to reporters at most media outlets. Financial problems led some journalists to rely more heavily on outside sources of income.

On August 20, the Union of Albanian Journalists condemned the so-called arbitrary dismissal of Alida Tota, news director at A1 TV, allegedly for reporting the August death of a 17-year-old boy working in the Sharra landfill near Tirana. A letter from the station owner to Tota published in the media stated that she was employed for an indefinite trial period and would be terminated from her position. Tota claimed she was dismissed because the Sharra story held the municipality of Tirana responsible for the conditions of child labor in the landfill.

<u>Libel/Slander Laws</u>: The law permits private parties to file criminal charges and obtain financial compensation for insult or deliberate publication of defamatory information. NGOs reported that the fines, which could be as much as three million leks ($24,000), were excessive and, combined with the entry of a conviction into the defendant's criminal record, undermined freedom of expression.

Internet Freedom

The government did not restrict or disrupt access to the internet or censor online content, and there were no credible reports the government monitored private online communications without appropriate legal authority. According to June data from Internet World Stats, 1.82 million persons, or approximately 60 percent of the population, used the internet. Approximately 35 percent of users accessed the internet through mobile telephones.

Academic Freedom and Cultural Events

There were no government restrictions on academic freedom or cultural events.

b. Freedom of Peaceful Assembly and Association

The constitution and law provide for the freedoms of assembly and association, and the government generally respected these rights.

c. Freedom of Religion

See the Department of State's *International Religious Freedom Report* at www.state.gov/religiousfreedomreport/.

d. Freedom of Movement, Internally Displaced Persons, Protection of Refugees, and Stateless Persons

The constitution and law provide for freedom of internal movement, foreign travel, emigration, and repatriation, and the government generally respected these rights.

The government cooperated with UNHCR and other humanitarian organizations in providing protection and assistance to refugees, returning migrants, asylum seekers, stateless persons, and other persons of concern. Police allowed UNHCR to monitor the processing, detention, and deportation of some migrants.

In-country Movement: In order to receive government services, individuals moving within the country must transfer their civil registration to their new community of residence and prove the legality of their new domicile through property ownership, a property rental agreement, or utility bills. Many persons could not provide this proof and thus lacked access to public services. Other citizens, particularly Roma and Balkan-Egyptians, lacked formal registration in the communities where they resided. The law does not prohibit their registration, but it was often difficult to complete. Many Roma and Balkan-Egyptians lacked the financial means to register, and many lacked the motivation to go through the process.

Protection of Refugees

Access to Asylum: The law provides for the granting of asylum or refugee status, and the government has established a system for providing protection to refugees.

There were credible reports from NGOs and migrants and asylum seekers that authorities did not follow due process obligations for some asylum seekers and that in other cases those seeking asylum did not have access to the system. Through October some 740 migrants and asylum seekers--mostly Afghans and Syrians-- entered the country. Authorities returned most to Greece, some immediately, others after weeks of detention in inadequate facilities. UNHCR was critical of the government's migrant screening and detention procedures, particularly in view of the increased presence of children among migrants. Through October authorities responded by transferring 18 migrants from the Karrec closed migrant detention facility to the Babrru open asylum center, where living conditions were much more family friendly. Authorities also housed more than a dozen migrants awaiting return to Greece in hotels in lieu of the Karrec center.

The law on asylum requires authorities to grant or deny asylum within 51 days of an applicant's initial request. Under the law, asylum seekers cannot face criminal charges of illegal entry if they contact authorities within 10 days of their arrival in the country. UNHCR reported that the asylum system lacked effective monitoring.

Safe Country of Origin/Transit: The law prohibits individuals from safe countries of origin or transit from applying for asylum or refugee status. UNHCR, however, reported that no asylum requests had been refused based on the government's list of safe countries, which includes Greece.

Employment: The law permits refugees access to work. The limited issuance of refugee identification cards and work permits, however, meant few refugees actually worked.

Access to Basic Services: The law provides migrants, asylum seekers, and refugees access to public services, including education, health care, housing, law enforcement, courts/judicial procedures, and legal assistance. Migrants and asylum seekers often required the intervention of UNHCR or local NGOs to secure these services.

Durable Solutions: In September the government completed the process of receiving Iranian Mujahedin-e Khalq refugees from Iraq and continued to facilitate their local integration throughout the year.

Temporary Protection: The government also provided subsidiary and temporary protection to individuals who may not qualify as refugees. As of October, the government was providing subsidiary protection to three persons and temporary protection to 24.

Stateless Persons

The number of stateless persons in the country was unclear. At the end of 2014, the most recent year for which statistics were available, UNHCR reported 7,443 stateless persons, most of whom were Romani or Egyptian children. According to UNHCR, 3,234 cases of statelessness have been resolved since 2011, but how many of these were part of the original 7,443 was unknown. Meanwhile, the risk of statelessness existed for unregistered children born abroad to returning migrant families and continued for Romani and Egyptian children. The law affords the opportunity to obtain nationality.

Section 3. Freedom to Participate in the Political Process

The constitution and law provide citizens the ability to choose their government in free and fair periodic elections held by secret ballot based on universal and equal suffrage.

Elections and Political Participation

Recent Elections: The most recent national parliamentary elections took place in 2013. The OSCE observer mission to the elections reported they "were competitive with active citizen participation throughout the campaign and genuine respect for fundamental freedoms." The OSCE further noted, "The atmosphere of distrust between the two main political forces tainted the electoral environment and challenged the administration of the entire electoral process."

In September a special election was held for mayor of Diber Municipality following the dismissal of the previous mayor for abuse of office. International observers assessed election-day events as calm and well run. In the weeks prior to the election, however, the process was marked by accusations of vote-buying and voter intimidation by both political parties.

In June 2015 the country held local elections nationwide for mayors and municipal councils. While offering a generally positive assessment of election-day events, the OSCE noted that the legal framework "could have provided the basis for democratic elections" but that the main parties misused their extensive powers and responsibilities and lacked the political will to implement the legal framework effectively. In its final report, the OSCE observer mission reported widespread allegations of pressure on voters, which, together with observed instances on election day, raised concerns about voters' ability to cast their vote freely. The observer mission also found the campaign environment to be peaceful, except for isolated incidents, and fundamental freedoms of expression and assembly were respected.

<u>Participation of Women and Minorities</u>: The participation of women in government steadily increased to a record of 23 percent women in parliament and 30 percent of ministers during the year. The law governing the 2013 parliamentary election required that 30 percent of candidates be women and that they occupy 30 percent of appointed and elected positions. According to the OSCE report on the elections, however, the three largest parties failed to meet the mandated 30 percent quota. The Central Election Commission fined these parties but nonetheless accepted their lists. The June 2015 local elections were held under a revised electoral code that requires parties to alternate male and female candidates on their lists. According to the OSCE final election report, women gained election to a greater proportion of places, approximately one-third, on local councils.

Civil registration requirements, including fees, and lack of identification made it difficult for many Roma to vote in the June 2015 local elections. Observers claimed that political parties offered to pay the registration fee in exchange for a vote. As of October, there were no Romani ministers or members of the Assembly.

Section 4. Corruption and Lack of Transparency in Government

The law provides criminal penalties for corruption by public officials, but the government did not implement the law effectively, and officials frequently engaged in corrupt practices with impunity. In December 2015 the Assembly approved decriminalization legislation preventing individuals with criminal convictions from serving as mayors, parliamentarians, or in government or state positions.

During the year authorities took additional steps to combat corruption. In July the Assembly unanimously approved constitutional amendments to approve a sweeping reform of the judiciary that included the creation of new anticorruption institutions. These included establishing an independent prosecutor's office and investigation unit, the sole responsibility of which will be the investigation and prosecution of high-level corruption and organized crime. In August the Assembly approved a law on vetting aimed at reducing corruption among prosecutors and judges. The government also expanded the use of body cameras on police officers to deter street-level corruption.

A number of government agencies investigated corruption cases, but limited resources, investigative leaks, real and perceived political pressure, and a haphazard reassignment system hampered investigations. The Ministry of Justice reported that convictions at district courts decreased by 37 percent in 2015 compared with 2014. No data was available with regard to the convictions at appeals courts. In selective instances involving international actors, anticorruption agencies cooperated with civil society.

Corruption: Corruption was pervasive in all branches of government. At the beginning of the year, 75 corruption cases were pending, with an additional 29 cases filed through June. Through August the courts convicted 76 defendants of corruption; 25 cases were dismissed. There remained 121 defendants charged with corruption awaiting trial. As of July, the web portal established in 2015 to allow citizens to report corruption by public officials had received 14,752 complaints, 94 of which the coordinator referred for prosecution.

While prosecutors made significant progress in pursuing low-level public corruption cases, including corrupt prosecutors and judges, prosecution of higher-level crimes remained elusive due to investigators' fear of retribution, a general lack of resources, and corruption within the judiciary itself. In September a court sentenced Spiro Ksera, a labor minister from the previous government, to 20 months in prison for abuse of office after he misappropriated 30 million leks ($240,000) meant to benefit the Romani community. In May authorities removed the mayor of the Dibra municipality, Shukri Xhelili, after broadcast of video footage in which he appeared to solicit sexual favors from a woman in exchange for a job. Xhelili appealed the decision to the Constitutional Court, which upheld his dismissal.

Financial Disclosure: The law requires public officials to disclose their assets to the High Inspectorate for the Declaration and Audit of Assets and Conflict of Interest (HIDAACI), which monitored and verified such disclosures and made them available to the public. During the year the number of HIDAACI inspectors investigating declarations of assets and conflicts of interest increased from 12 to 28. The law authorizes HIDAACI to fine officials who fail to comply with disclosure requirements or refer them to the prosecutor.

As of September, HIDAACI had fined 253 individuals, including ministers, deputy ministers, Assembly members, and heads of institutions for not disclosing their assets, for delaying their submissions, or for conflicts of interest. HIDAACI reported that by August it had referred 63 new cases for prosecution. These cases involved 13 judges, two prosecutors, seven Assembly members, two ambassadors, and 39 local government officials on charges including refusing to declare, hiding, or falsifying asset declarations, money laundering, falsification of documents, and corruption.

<u>Public Access to Information</u>: The law provides for public access to government information, but the government did not effectively implement the law. The process for making information public often was not clear, and officials were sometimes reluctant to release information. According to several NGOs, most information requests to ministries or municipalities were unanswered. The law stipulates that the right to access information can be restricted when information is categorized as classified or when such a release would violate the protection of personal data.

Most government ministries and agencies posted public information directly on their websites. Businesses and citizens complained that the process lacked transparency and that authorities failed to publish some regulations and legislation that should be basic public information. Citizens often faced serious problems obtaining such information. Individuals could generally access government information free of charge, but there were instances in which officials charged processing fees to cover the cost of service for the institution providing the information. Noncompliance is punishable as an administrative rather than a criminal offense. Citizens may appeal denials of disclosure to the authority with which they filed the original request or in a civil court.

Section 5. Governmental Attitude Regarding International and Nongovernmental Investigation of Alleged Violations of Human Rights

A number of domestic and international human rights groups generally operated without government restriction, investigating and publishing their findings on human rights cases. Government officials generally were cooperative and responsive to their views.

<u>Government Human Rights Bodies</u>: The Office of the Ombudsman is the main independent institution for promoting and enforcing human rights. The ombudsman is authorized by law to monitor and report on prisons and detention centers. The office may initiate an investigation in some cases where a victim is unable to come forward to do so. Although the ombudsman lacked the power to enforce decisions, he acted as a monitor for human rights violations. The Office of the Ombudsman was underfunded and understaffed. The ombudsman reported to

the Assembly annually. Although the Assembly distributed copies of some of the ombudsman's annual and special reports or posted them online, it rarely discussed the reports in plenary or committee sessions. The Assembly consulted the ombudsman's office on draft legislation related to human rights, but often this was only at the last minute or at the request of the ombudsman.

The Assembly has a committee on legal issues, public administration, and human rights.

Section 6. Discrimination, Societal Abuses, and Trafficking in Persons

Women

Rape and Domestic Violence: Rape, including spousal rape, is a crime. Penalties for rape and assault depend on the age of the victim. For rape of an adult, the prison term is three to 10 years; for rape of an adolescent between the ages of 14 and 18, the sentence is five to 15 years; and for rape of a child under 14, seven to 15 years. The law includes provisions on sexual assault and sexual harassment and makes the criminalization of spousal rape explicit. The government did not enforce the law effectively. Victims rarely reported spousal abuse, and officials did not prosecute spousal rape. The concept of spousal rape was not well understood, and authorities and the public often did not consider it a crime.

Domestic violence against women, including spousal abuse, remained a serious problem. Police often did not have the training or capacity to deal effectively with domestic violence cases.

Through August a government shelter for domestic violence survivors in Tirana assisted 24 women and 40 children, but it could not accept individuals without a court order. The government operated one shelter to protect survivors of domestic violence and NGOs operated four others. In addition, three NGO shelters provided protection and shelter to victims of trafficking as well as victims of abuse.

Sexual Harassment: The law prohibits sexual harassment, although officials rarely enforced it. NGOs and the commissioner for protection against discrimination believed sexual harassment was seriously underreported. The commissioner for protection against discrimination generally handled cases of sexual harassment. The commissioner may impose fines of up to 80,000 leks ($640) against individuals or 600,000 leks ($4,800) against enterprises.

<u>Reproductive Rights</u>: Couples and individuals have the right to decide the number, spacing, and timing of their children; manage their reproductive health; and have access to the information and means to do so, free from discrimination, coercion, or violence. The quality of and access to government-provided health care, including obstetric and postpartum care, was not satisfactory, especially in remote rural areas.

<u>Discrimination</u>: The law provides for the same legal status and rights for women as for men. Women were not excluded from any occupation in either law or practice, but in many fields, they were underrepresented at the highest levels. The law mandates equal pay for equal work, although many private employers did not fully implement this provision. In many communities, women experienced societal discrimination based on traditional social norms depicting women as subordinate to men. There were reports of discrimination in employment.

<u>Gender-biased Sex Selection</u>: According to the government's statistical agency, the ratio of boys to girls at birth in 2014 was 109 to 100, which indicated that gender-biased sex selection was possibly occurring. The government did not take any steps to address the imbalance.

Children

<u>Birth Registration</u>: An individual acquires citizenship by birth within the country's territory or from a citizen parent. Parents were encouraged to register the birth of a child in a timely manner, and the law provides for a monetary reward for parents who register their children within 60 days of birth. Often, however, authorities did not disburse the reward. There were no reports of discrimination in birth registration, but onerous residency and documentation requirements for registration made it more difficult for the many Romani and Balkan-Egyptian parents who lacked legally documented places of residence to register their children or to access government services dependent on registration.

According to the domestic branch of the NGO Association for the Social Support of Youth (ARSIS), children born to internal migrants or those returning from abroad, especially from Greece, frequently had no birth certificates or other legal documents and consequently were unable to attend school or have access to services. This was particularly a problem for Romani families, in which couples often married young and failed to register the births of their children.

<u>Education</u>: School attendance is mandatory through the ninth grade or until the age of 16, whichever occurs first, but many children, particularly in rural areas, left school earlier to work with their families. Parents must purchase supplies, books, uniforms, and space heaters for some classrooms; these were prohibitively expensive for many families, particularly Roma and other minorities. Many families also cited these costs as a reason for not sending girls to school. Although the government had a program to reimburse low-income families for the cost of textbooks, many families and NGOs reported they were unable to receive reimbursement after purchasing the books. NGOs noted that occasionally teachers discriminated against Romani children because of their perceived poor hygiene.

<u>Child Abuse</u>: Observers believed that child abuse was widespread, although victims rarely reported it. In 2013 the Children's Human Rights Center reported that 58 percent of children were victims of physical abuse, 11 percent were victims of sexual harassment, and almost 5 percent said they had been victims of sexual abuse. Almost 70 percent of children reported psychological abuse from family members, according to the center.

<u>Early and Forced Marriage</u>: Although the legal minimum age for marriage is 18, authorities did not enforce the law. Underage marriages occurred mostly in rural areas and within Romani communities. According to the 2015 *Early Marriages in Albania* study of the Observatory of Children, approximately 3 percent of children between the ages of 15 and 18 were married. The study also noted that 9 percent of Romani children between the ages of 13 and 18 were married. ARSIS claimed that, in certain Romani communities, girls as young as seven and boys as young as nine were considered married. Some NGOs reported that early and forced marriages occurred in rural communities as part of human trafficking schemes, with parents consenting to their underage daughters marrying older foreign men, who subsequently moved them to other countries.

<u>Sexual Exploitation of Children</u>: The penalties for the commercial sexual exploitation of a child range from eight to 15 years' imprisonment. The country has a statutory rape law, and the minimum age for consensual sex is 14. The penalty for statutory rape is a prison term of five to 15 years. In aggravated circumstances, the penalty may increase to life imprisonment. The law prohibits making or distributing child pornography; penalties are a prison sentence of three to 10 years. Possession of child pornography is illegal. The law explicitly includes minors in provisions that cover sexual abuse, harassment, exploitation for prostitution, benefiting from services offered by trafficked persons, facilitating trafficking, and domestic violence.

Authorities generally enforced laws against the rape and sexual exploitation of minors effectively, but NGOs reported that laws prohibiting child pornography were rarely enforced. Some children under the age of 18 were exploited for prostitution.

Displaced Children: There continued to be numerous displaced and street children, particularly in the Romani community. Street children begged or did petty work; some migrated to neighboring countries, particularly during the summer. These children were at highest risk of trafficking, and some became trafficking victims. Since the law prohibits the prosecution of children under 14 for burglary, criminal gangs at times used displaced children to burglarize homes. There were few prosecutions of child trafficking cases.

A 2014 study by the UN Children's Fund and Save the Children found that more than 2,500 children, nearly 75 percent of them from Romani or Balkan-Egyptian communities, begged or worked informally on the streets. Most children claimed earning money for their family was the principal reason for their begging or work, and nearly one-third of them said their parents forced them to work. According to the report, many of these children ran the risk of being trafficked.

The government subsequently implemented a pilot program in Tirana to remove children from the street and provide them with social care. Another pilot program provided financial incentives to parents to send their children to school and have them vaccinated. The State Agency for the Protection of Children's Rights reported that authorities assisted 345 out of 808 identified street children between July 2015 and June 2016. ARSIS reported that children continued to work in cannabis plantations around the country.

Institutionalized Children: Media reported on cases of child abuse occurring in the orphanages of Shkoder, Durres, and Saranda. In April the ombudsman investigated the Shkoder orphanage and recommended criminal charges against several members of the staff for physical and psychological abuse as well as exploitation of child labor. The investigation continued at year's end.

The migrant detention facility in Karrec was considered unsuitable for children, although a small number of migrant children resided there for periods lasting a few days to several weeks.

<u>International Child Abductions</u>: The country is a party to the 1980 Hague Convention on the Civil Aspects of International Child Abduction. See the Department of State's *Annual Report on International Parental Child Abduction* at travel.state.gov/content/childabduction/en/legal/compliance.html.

Anti-Semitism

There were reportedly only a few hundred Jews living in the country. There were no reports of anti-Semitic acts.

Trafficking in Persons

See the Department of State's *Trafficking in Persons Report* at www.state.gov/j/tip/rls/tiprpt/.

Persons with Disabilities

The constitution and laws prohibit discrimination against persons with physical, sensory, intellectual, and mental disabilities in employment, education, transportation, access to health care, the judicial system, and the provision of other state services. Nevertheless, employers, schools, health-care providers, and providers of other state services at times engaged in discrimination. The law mandates that new public buildings be accessible to persons with disabilities, but the government only sporadically enforced the law. According to the 2011 census, 24 percent of persons with disabilities had never attended school. Widespread poverty, unregulated working conditions, and poor medical care posed significant problems for many persons with disabilities.

In June the government approved the 2016-20 National Action Plan for Persons with Disabilities, supported by a state budget of 1.5 billion leks ($12 million). The government also funded the Albanian Disability Rights Foundation with five million leks ($40,000) for the production of wheelchairs. The government sponsored social services agencies to protect the rights of persons with disabilities, but these agencies traditionally lacked funding to implement their programs. Resource constraints and lack of infrastructure made it difficult for persons with disabilities to participate fully in civic affairs. Voting centers often were located in facilities lacking accommodations for such persons.

The ombudsman regularly inspected mental health institutions. Both the admission and release of patients at mental health institutions were problematic due to lack of sufficient financial resources to provide adequate psychiatric evaluations. There was societal discrimination and stigmatization of persons with mental and other forms of disability.

National/Racial/Ethnic Minorities

There were allegations of significant discrimination against members of the Romani and Balkan-Egyptian communities, including in housing, employment, health care, and education. Some schools resisted accepting Romani and Balkan-Egyptian students, particularly if they appeared to be poor. Many mixed schools that accepted Romani students marginalized them in the classroom, sometimes by physically setting them apart from other students.

Romani rights NGOs criticized the lack of legal safeguards against eviction and demolition of Romani camps included in the law on property legalization. Evictions and demolitions continued during the year and affected many Romani families. The government operated alternative housing programs for evicted families including Roma, but these programs were generally unsustainable without significant NGO and external donor support.

The law provides official minority status for both national and ethnolinguistic groups. The government defined Greeks, Macedonians, and Montenegrins as national groups; Greeks constituted the largest of these. The law defined Aromanians (Vlachs) and Roma as ethnolinguistic minority groups.

The ethnic Greek minority complained about the government's unwillingness to recognize ethnic Greek towns outside communist-era "minority zones" or to use Greek in official documents and on public signs in ethnic Greek areas. Public education was not available in the Romani, Serbo-Croatian, or Vlach languages.

Acts of Violence, Discrimination, and Other Abuses Based on Sexual Orientation and Gender Identity

The law prohibits discrimination based on sexual orientation, including in employment. Through August the government's commissioner for the protection against discrimination received five complaints from lesbian, gay, bisexual, transgender, and intersex (LGBTI) individuals and organizations. Enforcement of the law was generally weak. In May the Council Of Ministers adopted the National Plan of Action for the LGBTI 2016-20, and in August an order of the prime minister established the National Group of Implementation and Coordination to implement the action plan. The action plan seeks to improve the legal and institutional framework for protecting LGBTI persons; eliminate all forms of discrimination; and improve access to employment, education, health, and housing services.

Sexual orientation and gender identity are among the classes protected by the country's hate-crime law. Despite the law and the government's formal support for LGBTI rights, homophobic attitudes persisted in private and public life. Public officials sometimes made homophobic statements. NGOs reported that families evicted LGBTI persons from their homes during the year. Through August the country's first shelter for evicted LGBTI persons, opened in 2014, accommodated 12 individuals.

On May 14, activists participated in the fourth Tirana Gay (P)Ride against Homophobia, a short bicycle ride on Tirana's main boulevard, and Albanians witnessed the first television spot on family equality rights. As part of a "diversity festival," activists organized other activities, such as the public recognition of 30 persons who supported the LGBTI cause. Police ensured activists' safety during the events. In May the job placement company Headhunters Albania released an LGBTI employment equality index rating the compliance of private companies with recruitment laws that protect sexual orientation. The index of 71 companies indicated that 62 percent had inclusive human resource policies but only 3 percent specifically addressed nondiscrimination of LGBTI job candidates.

HIV and AIDS Social Stigma

The law prohibits discrimination against persons with HIV/AIDS. In the most recent demographic and health survey (2008-09), however, 71 percent of women and 69 percent of HIV-positive men reported discriminatory attitudes towards persons with HIV. Such persons experienced general social stigma, although there were no reports of violence against such individuals during the year.

Other Societal Violence or Discrimination

Incidents of societal killings, including both "blood feud" and revenge killings, occurred during the year. Media portrayed some gang-related killings as blood feud killings, and criminals at times used the term to justify their crimes. There were no cases of minors or women falling victim to blood feud killings. The ombudsman reported that authorities' efforts to protect families or prevent blood feud deaths were insufficient, although the government increased efforts to prosecute such crimes.

Section 7. Worker Rights

a. Freedom of Association and the Right to Collective Bargaining

The law and related regulations and statutes provide the right for most workers to form independent unions, conduct legal strikes, and bargain collectively. The law prohibits antiunion discrimination and provides for the reinstatement of workers fired for union activity. The law prohibits members of the military and senior government officials from joining unions and requires that a trade union have at least 20 members to be registered. The law provides the right to strike for all workers except uniformed military personnel, police, indispensable medical and hospital personnel, persons providing air traffic control and prison services, and both essential and nonessential workers in water and electrical utilities. Workers not excluded by their positions exercised their right to strike. These laws provided limited protection to domestic and migrant workers. Labor unions were generally weak and politicized. Workers who engage in illegal strikes can be compelled to pay for any damages due to strike action.

Government enforcement of these laws remained largely ineffective, in part due to the extent of informal employment. Resources for conducting inspections and remedying violations were not adequate. High fines, which under the law could reach 1.1 million leks ($8,700) or 50 times the monthly minimum wage, were rarely assessed. Fines were consequently not a sufficient deterrent to violations. Administrative and judicial procedures were subject to lengthy delays and appeals. Arbitration procedures allowed for significant delays that limited worker protections against antiunion activity.

Civilian workers in all fields have the constitutional right to organize and bargain collectively, and the law establishes procedures for the protection of workers' rights through collective bargaining agreements. Unions representing public-sector employees negotiated directly with the government. Effective collective bargaining remained difficult with employers opposed to union organizing and activities. In this environment, collective agreements, once reached, were difficult to enforce. Union leaders were sometimes dismissed due to political affiliation.

b. Prohibition of Forced or Compulsory Labor

The law prohibits all forms of forced or compulsory labor, but the government did not always effectively enforce the law. Lack of coordination among ministries and the sporadic nature of implementation of standard operating procedures hampered enforcement. Penalties of eight to 15 years in prison were sufficiently stringent to deter violations. Law enforcement organizations provided training to their officers in a victim-centered approach to human trafficking. The government continued to identify trafficking victims but prosecuted and convicted a small number of traffickers. The Office of the National Antitrafficking Coordinator increased government efforts to prevent trafficking through awareness activities.

There were instances of forced labor during the year. Children were subjected to forced begging and criminal activity (see section 7.c.).

Also see the Department of State's *Trafficking in Persons Report* at www.state.gov/j/tip/rls/tiprpt/.

c. Prohibition of Child Labor and Minimum Age for Employment

New amendments to the labor code effective in June set the minimum age of employment at 16 but allow children at the age of 15 to be employed in certain instances where the work is categorized as "light" and does not interfere with school. In general all children under the age of 18 may only work in jobs categorized as "light." By law the State Inspectorate for Labor and Social Services (SILSS), under the Ministry of Youth and Social Welfare, is responsible for enforcing minimum age requirements through the courts, but the SILSS did not adequately enforce the law. Labor inspectors investigated the formal labor sector, whereas most child labor occurred in the informal sector. The SILSS does not carry out inspections on child labor unless there is a specific complaint. Most labor inspections occurred in shoe and textile factories, call centers, and in retail enterprises; officials found some instances of child labor in the course of their inspections. Penalties were rarely assessed and were not sufficient to deter violations.

In 2013 the government's statistical agency and the International Labor Organization estimated that 54,000 children were engaged in forced labor domestically. An estimated 43,000 children worked in farms and fishing, 4,400 in the services sector, and 2,200 in hotels and restaurants. Nearly 7 percent of children were child laborers.

The law criminalizes exploitation of children for labor or forced services, but the government did not enforce the law effectively. The SILSS monitored for cases of child labor and other labor malpractices, but insufficient human resources limited its activities. There were reports that child laborers worked as street or shop vendors, beggars, farmers, shepherds, drug runners, vehicle washers, textile factory workers, miners, or shoeshine boys. Some of the children begging on the street were second- or third-generation beggars. Research suggested that begging started as early as the age of four or five. While the criminal code prohibits the exploitation of children for begging, police generally did not enforce the law, although they made greater efforts to do so during the year (see section 6, Displaced Children).

According to the State Agency on Children's Rights, between July 2015 and June 2016, authorities referred 24 parents to prosecutors for child abuse or exploitation, including forced labor. An investigation into the August death of a 17-year-old boy at the Sharra landfill revealed he had been working night shifts without a formal employment contract. The investigation also revealed that many other children were working under similar conditions and resulted in several arrests.

Also see the Department of Labor's *Findings on the Worst Forms of Child Labor* at www.dol.gov/ilab/reports/child-labor/findings/.

d. Discrimination with Respect to Employment and Occupation

Labor laws prohibit employment discrimination because of race, skin color, gender, age, physical or mental disability, political beliefs, language, nationality, religion, family, living with HIV/AIDS, and social origin. Discrimination in employment and occupation occurred with respect to gender, disability, sexual orientation and gender identity, nationality, and ethnicity.

e. Acceptable Conditions of Work

The national minimum wage was 22,000 leks ($176) per month. By comparison the national poverty threshold in 2013 was 6,874 leks ($55) per month. The law requires equal pay for equal work. The State Inspectorate for Labor and Social Services is responsible for enforcing the minimum wage. The inspectorate reported it had 113 inspectors, up from 110 in 2015.

While the law establishes a 40-hour workweek, individual or collective agreements typically set the actual workweek. The law provides for paid annual holidays, but only employees in the formal labor market had rights to paid holidays. Many persons in the private sector worked six days a week. The law requires payment of overtime and rest periods, but employers did not always observe these provisions. The law provides for premium pay for overtime. The government had no standards for a minimum number of rest periods per week and rarely enforced laws related to maximum work hours, limits on overtime, or premium pay for overtime, especially in the private sector. These laws did not apply to workers in the informal sector, such as domestic employees and migrant workers.

The SILSS is responsible for enforcing occupational health and safety standards and regulations. Enforcement was lacking overall. Workplace conditions in the manufacturing, construction, and mining sectors frequently were poor and, in some cases, dangerous. Resources and inspections were not adequate, and penalties of up to 50 times the monthly minimum wage of 1.1 million leks ($8,700) often did not deter violations, as law enforcement agencies lacked the tools to enforce collection and consequently rarely charged violators. There were no government programs to provide social protection for workers in the informal economy.

Violations of wage and occupational-safety standards occurred most frequently in the textile, footwear, construction, and mining industries. Workers often could not remove themselves from situations that endangered their health or safety without jeopardizing their employment. Employers did not effectively protect employees in this situation.